Jewels in the C Nazar~~tie~~

The LORD their God will save his people on that day as a shepherd saves his flock. They will sparkle in his land like jewels in a crown.
(Malachi 3:17, NIV)

Therefore God is not ashamed to be called their God, for he has prepared a city for them.
(Hebrews 11:16, NIV)

Life Story of Reverend Caiphas M. Mnisi

Contents

Preface

This book series celebrates the life stories of notable pastors and evangelists in the Church of the Nazarene. In 2010, the church celebrated 100 years since Rev. Harmon Schimelzenbach, *Sibhaha,* founded the first Mission of the Church of the Nazarene in Swaziland. Since then, God continues to raise a number of exemplary leaders in the Church. This is a tribute to these warriors of the Lord. It is also a challenge to us who have not yet crossed the river Jordan. The Scripture says (Hebrews 13:7, NLV): **"Remember your leaders, who first spoke God's Word to you. Think of how they lived, and trust God as they did."** *Kunjalo, indlela ibutwa kulabasembili* — we must follow the footsteps of conquerors.

The first book in the series "**Jewels in the Church of the Nazarene**" covers the life of Reverend Caiphas M. Mnisi, who served the Church as a pastor, church planter, and evangelist for more than five decades. He served the church as pastor from 1957 both in South Africa and Swaziland until his official retirement in 1989. In his post retirement, he formed the Mahenjane Church of the Nazarene for which he served as a pastor from 1997 up to the day he was called to be with the LORD on the 7th of February, 2013. He is fondly remembered for his teachings about Holiness. He constantly reminded the church that *"Siyawuhlangana ekuse---ni esangweni,"* all the Saints shall meet in the morning, just inside the Eastern Gate of the Holy City, the New Jerusalem.

May you be encouraged, strengthened, uplifted, and blessed as you read this biography. This is our prayer.

D. J. Shiba, B. F. Dlamini, and S.K. Mkhonta, July 2016

Acknowledgements

First, we thank God for the gift of life, health, and strength. This is the Lord's doing.

Our special gratitude goes to the Mnisi family: Maggie, Jean, Mandla, and their children. We are also indebted to the Mnisi family in Soweto, who gratefully welcomed us as part of the family and sharing with us intimate stories about their parents. *Siyabonga boMnisi wemvula!*

We also acknowledge a number of our brethren for their contributions. We are especially indebted to Pastor C. Pato and the elders at Mahenjane Church of the Nazarene. A major portion, if not all of Chapter 5 is a compilation of their testimonies. We are also grateful to a long list of brethren who took their time to share their testimonies about Rev. Mnisi. The list include among others Mrs. Elsie Gamedze, Mr. Bulunga, Rev. S. Lukhele, the Nothstine family, and the Gailey family.

Finally, we are grateful to Paul S. Dayhoff whose compilation of short biographies about Pioneers of the Church of the Nazarene is featured in the *"Dictionary of African Christian Biography"*. His work is referenced a number of times in this book.

Last but not least, we would like to thank Mrs. Dumsile Masuku for her editorial guidance and for her commitment to see that there was some merit in this book.

May God richly bless all of you.

Chapter 1

Birth and Upbringing

"For we are God's masterpiece. He has created us anew in Christ Jesus, so we can do the good things he planned for us long." (Ephesians 2:10)

Rev. Caiphas Masalesikhundleni Mboni Mnisi was born to Daniel Mahlakazane Mnisi and Maria Mhlabase Lukhele on April 20th, 1924 at eSigombeni (*eDlembeni*) in the central region of Swaziland. He was the last-born son in the family. His father gave him the name, *"Masalesikhundleni,"* meaning that he was the future leader of the family. His mother, a member of the Lutheran church at eMbekelweni, gave him the name Caiphas, the same name as the leading Jewish high-priest during of Jesus' public ministry.

As a kid, he used to accompany her mother to church but that did not mean much to him at that time. He was a very stubborn boy, who refused to do things without any conviction. For example, a traditional healer used to visit the family annually to ward off evil spirits at the beginning of the spring season. The traditional healer would burn incense prepared from animal skins and they were expected to inhale it and also spread the residues (*kuchela*) around their houses. He thought that was a myth and therefore he had to be coerced by his elder siblings to participate in this ritual.

In 1939, at the beginning of the Second World War,

King Sobhuza II made a call for each homestead to enlist at least one family member to the army to assist the British Allied Forces. Even though Caiphas was the youngest son in the family, he volunteered to represent his family. However, he was rejected by the authorities because of his age. This became a motivation later in his pastoral ministry because he felt that God preserved his life from world war so that he could be a soldier in the Lord's army.

Rev. Mnisi was also molded by the challenging environment around him. His father had seven wives, his mother being the fourth. He recalled that even though their mother was humble as a sheep and also treated their father as king, she was neglected the most. He said that *"lukhuni belutala umlotsa,"* meaning their mother's good conduct did not lead an obvious recognition. His mother's fields were often planted late leading to a poor harvest.

Career-wise, there was very little expected from them as children. Rev. Mnisi and his brothers were supposed to look after their father's cattle until they reached an age where they could go and work in the gold mines. His family also came from a lineage with royal responsibility. In 1840, king Mswati II asked the clan to look after his cattle behind the Mdzimba Mountains. As a teenager, he also got that opportunity to rear the royal herd at Lutfotja. He mentioned that this period was one the fruitful years of his life because he learned a number of practical skills about pastoral care out there in the woods.

In 1940, his parents were persuaded by a teacher from eMbekelweni Lutheran to send him to school. He enrolled at Zombodze National primary school. He became the first person in the family to set a foot at a school yard. He recalled that he left home for Zombodze wearing a loin skin and also carrying a homemade leather blanket. His parents had arranged for him to stay at a nearby homestead. However, some family members had reservations, and they felt that he was going to learn *bulumbi* (European corruption).

In those days, a vast portion of the country had been incorporated to South Africa. This land included farms that had been taken by European farmers through concessions with the Swazi authorities. The general public opinion was that the land was stolen. They were therefore worried that the European school education system will negate Swazi norms and values. Caiphas only studied at Zombodze for one month because the school closed after a teacher's strike. He then enrolled at eMbekelweni Lutheran primary; however, he did not have the opportunity to fully concentrate on his studies because he was also expected to assist his family in the fields.

Rev. Mnisi said that later in life, he cherished his early life experiences. Being born without a silver spoon meant that he could empathize with a number of people his ministry.

Chapter 2

Redemption and the Call to Ministry

Many are the plans in a person's heart, but it is the LORD's purpose that prevails. (Proverbs 19:21).

In 1944, Mnisi left eSigombeni to reside at her sister's marital home at eMbilaneni, in the southern part of Swaziland. He got the opportunity to finish his primary education supported by his brother in-law. This was also where he had enough quiet times to think and reflect about his career path.

One evening, he saw an uncommon bright shining star. In that moment he was engulfed with fear, such that he knelt down and prayed. In that midst, he saw a large crowd of people in great pain and suffering. They were calling him to show them a way out. After that incident, he had a heart for poor and frail people even though he was still not a Christian. First, he started to assist an old blind neighbor who lived alone. He would fetch water for her and tidy her yard. One day, he felt a small voice telling him to pray for her. After listening to the voice, he was amazed to see the woman gaining her sight. However, he did not think much about this miracle because he was preoccupied with his career prospects. In those times, it was an aspiration for most young Swazi men to work in the gold mines in Johannesburg.

In 1947, Mnisi left Swaziland for Durban, with a friend. After searching for jobs with no success in Durban, they eventually headed to Johannesburg where Mnisi was employed in the mines. He was a store-man for the dynamite supplies that were used to blow rocks underground. After a few months, he received news that his elder brother Philemon was living in the nearby at Jabavu, Soweto (Orlando West). The two brothers reunited and decided to stay together. Jabavu was an informal settlement for migrant workers. Their house was a shack built using *emasaka* (sacks). Caiphas recalled that they watched sunrise and sunset through their roof. At Jabavu he was employed at a Dry Clean store where he picked and delivered clothes to customers using a bicycle.

One afternoon, Caiphas met Rev. Gideon Nkambule, who was an evangelist at Jabavu Church of the Nazarene. This church had been planted by a Swazi pioneer missionary, Miss Salome Khumalo (Dayhoff', "Salome"). Rev. Nkambule invited him to the church services. He honored the invitation on a Sunday and found Rev. Nkambule preaching a sermon based on the scripture (Jeremiah 27:7): **"And I will send destroyers against you, everyone with his weapons, and they shall cut down your choice cedars, and cast them into the fire."**

Rev. Nkambule's main message was that arrogance leads to downfall. God opposes the proud and will discipline the arrogant. During the sermon, he repeatedly said that *"izokuwa imisedari yaseLebhanoni,"* the choice cedars of Lebanon will be cut down. Caiphas felt that axe of disgrace was hovering above his head; he needed to listen to the voice of God before it was too late. He gave his life to the Lord, soon after that sermon at the altar. Rev. Nkambule became his spiritual mentor.

In 1951, Caiphas saw the same vision he had seen four years back. He saw a bright light beckoning him to follow. Again, a great multitude in great pain and suffering were calling him to deliver them. This time, Rev. Nkambule became what Eli was to Samuel in the Old Testament. He advised him that this was God calling him to pastoral ministry.

Reflecting on how he met the Lord, he said that he would have never imagined that God could call someone in the midst of a fast-paced life of a city like Johannesburg. Indeed as the writer of Proverbs said "**A man's heart plans his way: but the LORD directs his steps**," (Prov. 16:9). We are the clay, God is the potter. We cannot escape His appointments and judgements but frustrate ourselves if we try to do so.

Chapter 3

South Africa: eJabavu and eJabulani

> *"But those who trust in the LORD will find new strength.*
> *They will soar high on wings like eagles.*
> *They will run and not grow weary.*
> *They will walk and not faint." (Isaiah 40: 31)*

In 1952, Caiphas got married to Miss Joana Kholiwe Msibi of Luhlokohla, Swaziland. She was also a member of Jabavu Church of the Nazarene. In 1955, the couple went to Siteki Bible College to prepare for ministry. In 1957, they completed their studies and returned back to Jabavu. At that time, the church was under the supervision of an American missionary, Rev. George Hayse and a local pastor Mr. Alpheus Nobela. Rev. Mnisi replaced Mr. Nobela who also went to Siteki Nazarene Bible College for training.

During the ministry at Jabavu, they embarked on a weekly door-to-door home visitation campaign in the neighborhood. They were soon drawn to a new settlement that was not served by any church. It was called eJabulani. Rev. Mnisi decided to start a roadside preaching point there. He would visit this preaching point midweek. To attract the attention, he would sing aloud the song: *"There is joy peace and happiness in my heart"* in vernacular. In the beginning only children came to listen to his sermons. He would teach them some short Bible lessons and then close the meeting with a prayer.

Rev D. Shiba (left) and Jean Mnisi (right) visiting at eJabulani Church of the Nazarene (Soweto) on November 16, 2014. This is first church Rev. Mnisi planted. The white house was the family residence from 1962 to 1969.

He kept a record of the number of children who attended the services. He was pleased when he saw that the numbers were increasing. Children were critical in his ministry, as they were to Jesus, our Lord. **Jesus said, "Let the little children come to me, and do not hinder them, for the kingdom of heaven belongs to such as these"** (Mat. 24:19). He recollected that he prepared thoroughly for the children service just like for any other church service. He would also visit their homes, to thank their parents for allowing them to attend his services.

The program was a success, some parents started to accompany their children to the service. Even street wanderers took some time to listen to his sermons. He recalled one Zulu old man who said after listening to his sermon, *"Cinisa kuloNkulunkulu, nguNkulunkulu mbamba lona.* (Hold on to this God, your God is real.)" What struck him was that this man was well-known in the area as a staunched traditionalist.

In 1958, the roadside preaching point was formally established as a church. In 1959, Rev. George Hayse oversaw the construction of the church structure with funds sourced from the Alabaster fund (Chapman, 1959). He then appointed another pastor to relieve Rev. Mnisi, who was to remain at Jabavu. However, in 1962, Rev. Mnisi was called to return to the church after it developed serious issues.

They were allegations that the pastor's wife was unfaithful. Some church members had caught her committing adultery with another member during an all-night prayer service. Things escalated when the pastor also became an alcoholic. People withdraw from the church and also did not want their kids to be associated with it. Directing a revival for such a church was a daunting task because of negative publicity it had attracted.

Their first strategy was to visit those who had never attended church before. Again, in the beginning only children responded to their invitations. These children came from faraway places and Mrs. Mnisi would offer them a light meal after the Sunday service. A turning point in their ministry occurred when Rev. Mnisi volunteered to lead a funeral service in the area. A lot of people in the community were moved by his message. News also spread around that Mnisi was not paid for the service. This was contrary to what was happening in Soweto in those days since church leaders charged a fee to lead a funeral.

Rev. Mnisi became the pastor of the community and he also connected with many people through his home visitations. He also visited bereaved families in community as soon as possible to offer his condolences. He never waited to be invited. Many souls were lead to Jesus Christ through these programs.

As the church grew in numbers, Rev. Mnisi would often conduct mid-week revival services to speak about the tenets of the Christian faith. They would start from Wednesday and end on Sunday. He led the revivals himself without inviting a guest speaker.

At times the evening services where chaotic because the church was located in a rough neighborhood. He shared one incident of an intoxicated man once attended these services. On the first day, this man was disruptive. He came back on the next day and continued to be noisy. On the third day, he returned carrying a can of coca cola. He told the congregation that it was present for Rev. Mnisi, recognition of his resilient efforts. On the last day, this man gave his life to Christ and became a devoted member of the church. Mnisi said that from that incident, God taught him not to discount any souls seeking after Christ, *nobe imabokoboko*—though they may be deranged and flimsy.

Church growth did not mean that the family had it easy. The church was located in what was one of the most impoverished parts of Soweto. The church budget was almost non-existent. The family's only income was a monthly stipend from the District, just enough to buy a bar of soap, a bag of sugar (5 kg) and a bag of mealie meal (25 kg). He recalled that there were days when they ate the same thing, *lipalishi nemanti ashukela* (corn meal) during breakfast, lunch, and dinner. These living conditions were also experienced by several native pastors in that district.

Rev. Mnisi together with other nine local pastors decided to approach the then Regional Director (Africa region) Rev. Dr. William Esselstyn *(Masithulele)*, to seek for more support. Rev. Esselstyn made it clear that the district could not afford to increase their allowances. After this meeting, five pastors decided to engage in secular pursuits and resigned from ministry. Some decided to join other denominations with better working conditions. But Rev. Mnisi decided to stay put, as he could not desert a church he had planted. He asked himself this question **"For what will it profit a man if he gains the whole world, and loses his own soul?"** (Mark 8:36, NKJV).

He also decided to organize a four days revival to teach about tithing and giving. After the revival, he placed a container behind the church door and asked the church to put any food stuffs or second-hand clothes that he could distribute to the poor and for his family. This container became widely known as the pastor's box and was adopted by a number of church through-out South Africa. To this day it is practiced in many local churches including those in Swaziland as way to support the local pastor's family. People also began bringing tithes to the church. He said the song *"Ngenisani kweshumi kwaJehova* (Bring in the sheaves)" became the church anthem for collecting tithes and offerings.

God also provided for the family in special ways, he recounted that he had a beautiful shirt that he wore for many years. He mentioned that from that time he learned that God can make the clothes to last as long as necessary, just as He did so for the children of Israel in the wilderness (Deuteronomy 8:4): **"Your clothes did not wear out and your feet did not swell during these forty years [in the wilderness]."**

We asked him if he ever organized all-night services after what happened in Jabulani. He gave us a quick and short response: *lidlojwa kanye lesabe* (once hurt [the eye] it is always in fear). He said that from that moment, he was concerned about the unintended consequences of all-night prayer meetings. Even when they became very popular amongst other denominations, he continued to have some reservations.

Rev. Mnisi concluded his ministry in South Africa in 1969 after spending five and seven years at Jabavu and Jabulani, respectively. That same year, he received a letter from Siteki Church of the Nazarene asking him to return to home. After two weeks of prayer, Mnisi agreed with Rev. G. Hayse encouraging him to follow his calling.

Chapter 4

Siteki Church of the Nazarene

> *And how will anyone go and tell them without being sent?*
> *(Romans 10:15a, NLT)*

In 1969, Rev. Mnisi and his family returned to Swaziland to lead the Church of the Nazarene (Fitch Memorial church) in Siteki. He replaced Rev. Leonard Sibandze, who became the District Superintendent. This was a diverse congregation. The mission served three institutions: a Bible College, a school, and a clinic. The church membership included oversea missionaries, student pastors, school children, teachers, nurses, and members of the community. Rev. Mnisi was also expected to play an administrative role in these institutions.

Dr. Charles Gailey and his wife, who were then part of the congregation, recalled that Rev. Mnisi and his family settled down very well. They quickly endeared themselves to everyone in Siteki. People realized that he was a powerful preacher, but more than that—an upright, moral man who "walked the talk". He was a man of prayer, and a mentor to student pastors. He used to organize prayer meetings for student pastors every Saturday morning at 8:30 AM. After the prayer meeting, he would organize them into small teams to go for door-to-door home visitations. Each group was expected to compile a report about their outreach session. Many people gave their lives to the Lord as a result of this program. It led to the establishment of a number of churches including Makhewu, Mlindazwe, Tikhuba, Maphungwane, and Maphatsindvuku.

Former students of the Bible College were also inspired by his mentorship style. He was a leader who led by example. He treated them as equals. They recalled that he used to remind them that *"Lolokubitile wangibita nami, luhloniphe lubito* (we were called by the same God, honor the call)". Rev. Star Lukhele stated that Mnisi was a leader who accommodated all ages in his ministries. He mentioned Rev. Mnisi's habit of carrying two handkerchiefs in his pocket, one for him and the other that he used to keep children clean.

Students in at Siteki Bible College in the 1950s.

Rev. Mnisi's life also touched a number of missionaries who worked at Siteki. Siphiwe Carol Gailey, the daughter of Charles Gailey, testified that one evening she heard Rev.

Mnisi preaching a powerful sermon on sanctification and holiness based on Romans 12:1-2: "**Therefore, I urge you, brothers and sisters, in view of God's mercy, to offer your bodies as a living sacrifice, holy and pleasing to God—this is your true and proper worship....**"

On that evening at home she thought and prayed about those verses. In that very evening she surrendered her life to God's will. Her life changed ever since. Her brother Dr. Robert Gailey also acknowledged the influence of Rev. Mnisi in his life. He said that he became successful in life because "he sat under the ministry of Rev. Mnisi". Their friend, Dan Miller, was nick-named Jabulani Mnisi because of Rev. Mnisi. Dan was very proud of that name because it associated him to a man of integrity and honor. Another missionary, Rev. T Nothstine testified that he felt fortunate to have worked with Rev. Mnisi. To him, he was a pattern for Christlikeness for all in church.

Rev. Mnisi also assumed administrative roles at the primary and secondary schools. He teamed up with Mr. Norman Vilakati, who was then the principal of Siteki Secondary School. Norman was also a member of the church board. The two men shared mutual respect between themselves. Rev. Mnisi was impressed about the great ideas Norman had for the Nazarene schools. The partnership only lasted for five years as in 1975 Norman went to work for the Swazi embassy in the USA.

Rev. Mnisi with Pastor Philemon Lukhele. The SD 372 CL was the Mnisis family van.

The couple with their missionaries: Rev. T. Nothstine and his wife L. Nothstine

Rev. Mnisi then linked up with Mr. Shongwe who took over Norman. They also developed an excellent working relationship. Rev. Mnisi was concerned about the spiritual life of the students at the secondary school. He found that most students who went to pursue their higher education elsewhere lost their faith. He prayed for the extension of the school to form 5. His prayers were answered in 1976, when the school received a grant from the World Bank via the Ministry of Education to build more classrooms. However, some church authorities were not comfortable on the involvement of a "worldly" institution within the Mission. The new classes were built at a distance from those built by missionaries. These developments led to the current Siteki Nazarene high school.

The Mnisi family was loved and respected by the church and the community. Mrs. Elsie Gamedze a member of the church said that they loved the Mnisis for unleashing the best for God and for honesty. Mnisi taught them about the ministry of home visitations. Mr. Bulunga, a teacher at Siteki Nazarene High School was one of those people who accompanied Mnisi to Good Shepherd Hospital to visit the patients there. He testified that his association with the Mnisi family enriched his walk with the Lord. He recalled that Mnisi used to salute people by saying *"Manibusiswe nguJehova* (May you be blessed by Jehovah)." He said that these days he has increasingly understood the deep spiritual meaning of this benediction, especially, since it resonates with Psalms 115:14-15: **"May the LORD cause you to flourish, both you and your children. May you be blessed by the LORD, the Maker of heaven and earth."** Indeed, this is a generous benediction since both great and small need his blessing to flourish.

Mnisi also taught the church how to acknowledge gifts. He told them to say *"Ngcwele, Ngcwele, Ngcwele (Holy, Holy, and Holy)."* He said that this was how angels salute God in Heaven. This slogan has been adopted by a number of pastors in the church as a way to express their appreciation. Rev. Mnisi would also interject his sermons with the proclamation *"Siyawuhlangana ekuse---ni eSangweni. (we* shall meet in the morning just inside the Eastern *Gate.)"* This was his way to create nostalgia about Heaven.

Rev. Mnisi also worked with number of people outside the Church of the Nazarene. He subscribed to the principles of Church: "We [the Nazarenes] are blood-brothers to every blood-bought, blood-washed soul in the universe," (Gene, 1983).

In the 1980s, he developed a close relationship with Father Morris who was the priest at Good Shepherd Catholic Mission. This relationship enabled him to be the first non-Catholic pastor to be allowed to preach at Good Shepherd Hospital wards. He would be also invited to lead Morning Prayer sessions for the hospital employees. Rev. Mnisi would also visit Lubombo Central High School (a public school). He would preach to the students for less than five minutes at the morning assembly. Many souls were won back to God in this campaign. Former students recalled that no one wanted to miss out Tuesdays' morning assembly because Mnisi always began his short sermons with anecdotal stories. He once told them a story of a raven (*lohheya*) and a tortoise (*lufudvu*). He said

"Once upon a time a raven became a friend of a tortoise. One day, the raven invited the tortoise to a dinner in a place far away. Since the tortoise could not fly, so the ravel decided to carry his friend with a string tied around the tortoise's body. The raven lifted his friend with a string in its mouth. On their way, they came across a group of children playing. The children were amazed to see a raven flying with a tortoise. They started to tease them. The raven was so upset, that it decided to rebuke these kids. Unfortunately, it had to open its mouth and in the process the poor tortoise slipped down in a free fall. It hit the ground breaking into pieces."

The moral lesson of the story was that the students must choose their friends wisely. They should always read the moral character of the people they meet along the way and not to be over trusting just like what the tortoise did.

The Mnisis retired from Siteki in 1989 after reaching the official retirement age of 65 years. Mnisi's final word about his life of ministry with his wife Joan was: "I thank God who led us in his work, and not only that, he also took care of us while we worked in his field, and it is sweet to walk with Jesus." He promised to intercede for the church just as the prophet Samuel promised Israel at the coronation of King Saul (1 Samuel 12:23): "**Moreover as for me, God forbid that I should sin against the LORD in ceasing to pray for you.**"

From 1989 to 1997, Mnisi and his wife continued to worship at Siteki Church of the Nazarene. The old couple was known for punctuality and time keeping. They arrived in all the services earlier than most of the people. Sometimes they would wait outside until the one with the church keys will open for them. They used to be reported in case they were not attending.

Chapter 5

Mahenjane Church of the Nazarene

"He shall be like a tree planted by the rivers of water that brings forth its fruit in its season, whose leaf also shall not wither; And whatever he does shall prosper."
(Psalms 1:3, NKJV)

The first part of the book of Joshua ends with a list of thirty one kings that were conquered by Joshua in the land of Canaan (Joshua 12: 7-24). To as much success that he had achieved, there was still a lot to be done. The second part of the book begins with LORD speaking to Joshua. He said (Joshua 13:1): **"You are old, advanced in years, and there remains very much land yet to be possessed."** Rev. Mnisi realized the same facts upon his retirement years. A number of congregations around Siteki lacked fulltime pastors. Paul said (Romans 10:14):`` **How then can they call on the one [Jesus] they have not believed in? And how can they believe in the one of whom they have not heard? And how can they hear without someone preaching to them?"** Rev. Mnisi felt he could not use old age as an excuse, a faithful servant never retires.

In 1997, at the age of 73 years, Rev. Mnisi came out of retirement to establish Mahenjane Church of the Nazarene by combining three preaching points that were under Rev. Gladys M. J. Dlamini from Maphatsindvuku. Rev. Mnisi used the public transport to travel to and from Siteki to lead the Sunday Service at Mahenjane. They group met under a big tree by the roadside. His services attracted a number of people. Few months later they had to build a temporary structure that could shelter them on rainy days.

In 1998, the local area council allocated them land next to an abandoned homestead of *inyanga*. The church members were eager for a permanent church building. People donated building materials and Mnisi's grandson (Kenneth Maziya) drew a church building plan. The church prayed at the site before the foundation cornerstone was laid. Rev. Gideon Mnisi led a team of builders who had volunteered. In 2003, the walls were completed and a self-fund raising campaign for the roofing started. A church elder recalled that Rev. Mnisi told them that nobody was going to feed their elephant. They had to finish it off.

That same year their precious elephant was swept away. A heavy storm swept Mahenjane and utterly destroys the church building. The first people who saw the damage were shaken. Mrs. Mhlanga (laNkhosi) who was one of them said "What made it especially difficult was that we were worried how Rev. Mnisi would take the news since he was not in good health at that time." Nevertheless God gave them the courage to call him. She recalled that after he heard the news, his first words were: *"Makabongwe Nkulunkulu* (Praise be to God)." He went on to comfort them that God was ever present.

Rev Mnisi at the beginning of his ministry at Mahenjane. Next to him is Rev. Dlamini who succeeded him as pastor at Siteki Nazarene and the then District Superintendent Rev. Malambe.

On the first Sunday after the storm, Rev. Mnisi requested church members to seek the counsel of God through fasting. He requested both the young and old to participate. He went on to preach a sermon based on the prophecy of Jeremiah (Jeremiah 29:11): **"For I know the thoughts that I think towards you, says the LORD, thoughts of peace and not of evil, to give you a future and a hope."** He told them that they serve a Mighty God who could build his temple without using their cheap bricks of mortar and clay.

In a church board meeting Rev. Mnisi was requested to ask for assistance from the then Prime Minister of Swaziland, a son of a renowned Nazarene preacher. But he asked them to wait for the LORD. The news of the storm reached Mr. Ken P. Walker, a close friend of the Mnisi family. Ken organized funds from the Nazarene Mission International to rebuild the church.

In 2005, Mr. Walker and a team of builders from the USA arrived with building materials. The team worked tirelessly for days and restored the church within few weeks. The new building was bigger and better. The construction happened so quickly that some people thought that God had sent angels to fulfil Rev. Mnisi's prophecy. That same year, Rev. Mnisi celebrated his 81st birthday. People were amazed how God was using his servant even at such an advanced age.

Rev. Mnisi spent the next eight years actively leading the church. He acknowledged in our interview that there were times when he felt his body could not take him to where he wanted to go, but his heart was always on the work of God. He wanted to be at the battle field as long as he was still effective in his work.

On the 3rd of February 2013, Rev. Mnisi preached his last sermon at the church. February is the youth month in the church calendar. Ncamsile Sigwane reported that Rev. Mnisi began his sermon with these words: "I have pleaded with God to grant me this opportunity to preach to you young people. I cannot ask Him for more. If am raptured afterwards, it is well with me." He asked the congregation to read Ecclesiastes 10: 9: **"Rejoice, O young man, in your youth, and let your heart cheer you in the days of your youth; Walk in the ways of your heart, And in the sight of your eyes; But know that for all these God will bring you into judgment. "**

The focus of his message was on purity. He told them that "hurry, hurry has no blessings, but patience leads to joy." He challenged them to preserve their bodies for holy marriage since they were the temple of the Holy Spirit. Immediately after giving the sermon, he fell ill. That evening, he got admitted at Good Shepherd Hospital in Siteki. Four days later he went home to rest with the Lord.

The church was shocked with his immediate passing but also celebrated his exemplary life. Condolences came from people all over the world: America, Britain, Kenya, South Africa, and Mozambique to name but a few countries. Indeed, a great soldier of the Lord was called from the battle field after conveying his message to the next generation.

Chapter 6

Parenthood

> *"For every house has a builder, but the one who built everything is God." (Hebrews 3:4, NLT)*

In 1951, Rev. Mnisi met his wife Joana Msibi at Jabavu Church of the Nazarene, Soweto. They were both members of the church. Mnisi was preparing to go to Bible school to prepare for ministry. He recalled that in those days he was asking God to provide him with a suitable helpmate. He had pleaded with the Lord: "If you would give me a good wife, I will shepherd your flock."

God answered his prayer with Joana, a fellow Swazi from Luhlokohla, in Manzini. She did her primary education at Manzini Nazarene and her secondary school at a Methodist school in KwaZulu-Natal. She had worked as nursing assistant at Manzini Nazarene hospital before coming to Jabavu.

A year later, the couple got married in Manzini after Mnisi had paid *lobola*. The couple was blessed with four children, three daughters: Maggie, Jean and Joyce (twins), and a son Mandla. In 1955, the couple went together for training in pastoral ministry in Siteki Bible College. They testified that they experienced great blessings early on their ministry at Siteki during home visitations as they led a number of people to the Lord. In 1957, they completed their studies and returned to Jabavu.

Their children recollected their fond memories of growing up as preacher's kids. They recalled that they were raised with love and strict discipline. Their father was the disciplinarian, but both parents supported each other when they were being disciplined. They remembered that their father would always call the offender to a separate room for a 'pre-punishment counselling' session. He would open the bible and read the scriptures including: Proverbs 13: 24 **"He who spares his rod hates his son, But he who loves him disciplines him promptly,** " Proverbs 29:15: **"The rod and rebuke give wisdom, but a child left to himself brings shame to his mother,"** and Hebrews 12 12:7-11 : **"...for what son is there whom a father does not chasten..... Now no chastening seems joyful for the present, but painful; nevertheless, afterwards it yields the peaceable fruit of righteousness to those who have been trained by it. "** A punishment followed after that.

Maggie recalled that their home was not a loose kraal -- *kwampuzi idlemini, kwamacanca.* They were expected to report back home before 5 PM. On Saturdays, they were expected to clean the house and wash their school uniforms. Sundays were reserved for worship, nothing else. Their father was passionate about ensuring that kept Sunday as a Sabbath day. She recalled an incident at Siteki involving some overseas missionaries. They were completing a building project on a Sunday. Their father approached the missionaries to admonish them to stop working on Sundays. They had no option but to stop. So the Sunday's policy was not only for the parsonage but their father tried to promote it throughout the Nazarene Mission.

Rev. Mnisi and his wife, Joana in the early years of their ministry.

The couple with Isabel Simelane (nee Ndwandwe) who was a matron of Siteki Bible College at the time.

Rev. Mnisi began his day at 5 AM with a prayer. The children enjoyed listening to his prayers, especially, since he often made special prayers for each member in the family. So they wanted to hear what he was saying to God about each one of them. They also saw how their father loved their mother. Maggie joked that some of them rushed to get married because they envied the life of their parents. Their parents never argued in front of them. They always excused themselves and go to their bedroom to discuss family issues.

Reflecting on their mother, they said she embraced all the attributes of a virtuous wife found in Proverbs 31:10-31. During trying times, early in their father's pastoral ministry, their mother ensured they never go to school hungry.

The children also admitted that life for them as preacher's kids was not always rosy because they at times felt like they were living in a glass house. They were open to public scrutiny because people expected them to conduct themselves just-like their parents. They also often struggled to make genuine relationship with people from the church. They too experienced temptations just like any other kid in the church. Each one of them went through a period of rebellion. They did so not to hurt their parents or to disgrace the church. In those trying times, they were encouraged by the love their parents had for them, which they also extended to the church. Through it all, each one of them found his or her way back to the Lord. Currently, Maggie and Jean are active members of the Church of the Nazarene. Mandla is an active member of the Apostolic Faith Mission.

The Mnisi family at 50th anniversary of Rev. Mnisi and his wife. From left to right: Jean, Mandla, Musa Maziya, Maggie, Joyce, Gabsile Luhlanga.

In 2002 the couple celebrated their 50 year wedding anniversary in a grand ceremony that brought together retired pastors, friends and family members. Rev. Mnisi told the congregation that the secret of a long happy marriage was that couples should maintain humor. They should have time to play together and also maintain family prayer time.

The couple at the wedding of their grand-daughter Sihle Mnisi.

The family also went through rough times. In 2004 Joyce, Jean's twin sister, passed away timeously when Rev. Mnisi and his wife were in Durban in a church trip for retired pastors. This was one of the most trying times for the couple more so because at that time Joyce was staying with them. They were old and therefore looked up to Joyce as their nurse. In such times, they found comfort from counting the many blessings in their lives.

Rev. Mnisi and his wife in during their 50th anniversary. Rev. Pato on the left.

Babe and make Mnisi.

The 50th wedding anniversary party. From left to right: Mrs. Lomafu Pato, Rev. Michael Zewula, Mrs. Dlamini (laSithole), Rev. Sunlight Dlamini, Mrs. Miriam Bhembe, Rev. Moses Mnisi, and Mrs. Miriam Mnisi

The couple receiving a blessing. Rev Mahlalela with microphone, Rev. Malambe next to him. On the far-right are Rev. James Dlamini and also Dr. Hynd can be identified behind the couple.

In the last days of their lives, the couple was very much inseparable and they also wished that it could be so even when they sleep in the grave. Few weeks before Rev. Mnisi passed on, he told his brother's son Vusi that he wanted to be buried on the same tomb with his wife at Sigombeni. He also asked his son Mandla, he should take care of his mother. He then gave him his favorite brown suit and said he should wear this suit on their mother's graduation day, her funeral.

When Rev. Mnisi went on to be with the Lord on the 7th of February 2013, the children feared about the health of their mother. The church joined together and prayed for her strength. Indeed, she attended the funeral service of her husband. A year later, on the 24th of October 2014, Rev. Shiba went to visit *make* Mnisi. She found her in good spirit. Make Mnisi asked that they sing together the song: *"Uyamangalisa Jesu, usitselele izono zethu (I am amazed that Jesus loves me)."*

She then said she always felt her husband's love as if they had just married yesterday. Mrs. Mnisi went on to be with the Lord on the 4th of November, 2015. She was buried next to her husband.

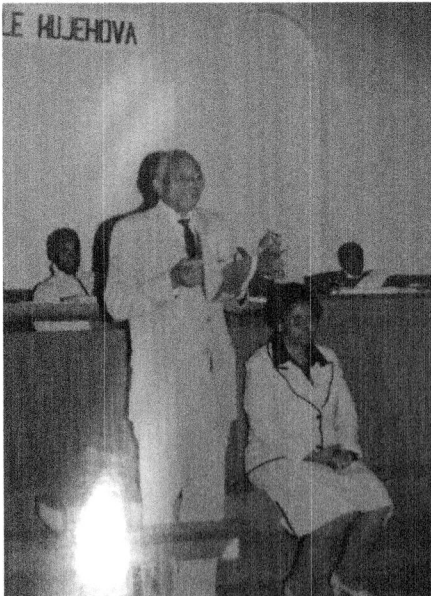

Rev Mnisi and his wife at a church service.

The couple in Durban at the retired pastors' retreat in 2010.

Rev. D. Shiba graduation ceremony in 1991, with *babe* and *make* Mnisi.

Jean dancing with her father during their parent's 50th anniversary in 1992.

Chapter 7

Guidance for the Young

> *"Hear, my children, the instruction of a father, and give attention to know understanding. For I give you good doctrine...." (Proverbs 4:1-2)*

Rev. Mnisi served as a pastor in the Church of Nazarene for six decades. With such a wealth of experience, he was regarded as a walking library by many people. Students from the Siteki Nazarene Bible College would often consult him for their final year research papers. They all testified about his spirit of oneness. He often told them that *"Lolokubitile wangibita nami, luhloniphe lolubito,"* meaning that they were to remember that both senior and junior pastors would be judged on the same standards.

Below is a general list of advices Rev. Mnisi felt could help to guide a young minister in his or her mission:

1) **Go!** Go out there, meet people and tell them about the love of God. The "job description" of a servant of God is to go and share the gospel. Do not avoid the poverty stricken places. **"Go out into the country lanes and out behind the hedges and urge anyone you find to come, so that the house will be full"** (Luke 14:13). Share the good news with anyone, anywhere: in their homes, in the hospitals, and prisons. Tell them that God cares and loves them.

2) **Be ready to take notes**. Carry a notepad with

you. God speaks at any time. Sometimes in just one word. One of the best lesson, I learned from Bible College is that a written message even with a loose handwriting is better than a memory that can be easily forgotten. The most powerful message can come from reflecting and connecting the dots in your notepad with prayer and discernment. The written word is powerful. That is why God often asked his prophets to write things down. He said to Habakkuk (Habakkuk 2:2): **"Write my answer plainly on tablets, so that a runner can carry the correct message to others."**

3) **Holiness**. Sing it, preach it, and live it. Be aware of the traps that can destroy your ministry, especially pride, materialism, idle talks, and sexual immorality. *Ungacoshani nemali*--never compromise the truth for money. Be satisfied with your portion as a Levite. Surely, if you stand on the word of God, goodness shall follow you. Work in the open; avoid dark corners that can make you vulnerable to the enemy. In my ministry I saw a big church destroyed by adultery that occurred in the dark corners during an "all-night prayer" meeting.

4) **Keep time**. Punctuality is the courtesy of kings, but we are servants not kings, we have to value people's time. As a pastor you have the platform to set the right pace at which things get done in the church. Even an organized congregation gets demotivated if its leader does not respect their time. *Likhonyane lempunzi leca lakwece unina khona*—followers cannot outshine their leader. I developed a habit of arriving fifteen minutes earlier in all my appointments. This has helped me to be always on time.

5) **Read your church.** Do not despise the former pastor your congregation. This can divide the church.

Every community has its own challenges--*akukho mfula ungahlokomi.* You are called to nurse every sheep in the kraal, you are responsible for all. Remember Jesus has called us to be good shepherds. A shepherd who will sacrifice his life for even the least in the herd.

6) **Wait for the Lord.** Take the long view of issues. *Inhlwa ayibanjwa ngenhloko isavela--*the winged terminate is not caught by its head as soon as it appears; wait until you get the whole story before you can act. You will receive a number of invitations and appointments, rely on God. Do not rush to accept a new appointment until God confirms it.

7) **Train your Timothy.** As much as possible, do not do ministry alone. Empower others to assist you in your ministry and evangelism campaigns. Good seeds multiply. Excellent leaders produce others, Moses nurtured Joshua and Paul nurtured Timothy.

Rev. Mnisi shared to us these great points with a heart to equip young pastors. He supported the writing of this book for the same reasons. He was also honored by the Lord, that he got the opportunity to preach his last message to young people in the church. In his last meeting with his daughter Jean, he also asked her to read the following verses at his memorial service as his final message to his colleagues:

"These words are from my heart to you. I say this before God and Jesus Christ. Some day He will judge those who are living and those who are dead. It will be when Christ comes to bring His holy nation.

Preach the Word of God. Preach it when it is easy and people want to listen and when it is hard and people do not want to listen. Preach it all the time.

Use the Word of God to show people they are wrong. Use the Word of God to help them do right. You must be

willing to wait for people to understand what you teach as you teach them.

The time will come when people will not listen to the truth. They will look for teachers who will tell them only what they want to hear.

They will not listen to the truth. Instead, they will listen to stories made up by men. You must watch for all these things. Do not be afraid to suffer for our Lord. Preach the Good News from place to place. Do all the work you are to do." (2 Timothy 4: 1-5, NLV).

Chapter 8

An Undivided Heart

> *"Teach me your way, LORD, that I may rely on your faithfulness; give me an undivided heart, that I may fear your name."*
>
> *(Psalms 86:11)*

Rev. Mnisi is remembered for being a single-minded person, who wanted nothing else but to preach the gospel. He declined a number of promotions to other pastoral offices because he felt they would steal his time for home visitations and personal evangelism.

Early in his ministry in Jabavu, Rev. Mnisi was nominated by the then Missionary Rev. Heyse to be a certified marriage counselor but he declined. Fellow pastors were amazed because this assignment came with an extra income. However, Rev. Mnisi had the perception that marriage counselling was going to take too much time for his pastoral duties. Rev. Mnisi was also nominated to become the District Superintendent for Swaziland East district to succeed Rev. L. Sibandze. But once again he declined. His excuse was that *"Mine ngibetelwe kushumayela."* He meant that God had called him to preach to the people on the streets.

In the 1970s, he was asked to teach a course on Evangelism at Siteki Bible College. He found it hard to focus solely on lectures. A story is told that in one of his classes, a great fire of spiritual revival occurred. It started when he was teaching about the "Life of a Christian." It was a great revival such that classes had to be suspended for a week, as some students were praying non-stop in the lecture halls and others confessing their sins. One of the students who witness that revival is Rev. Gladys M. Dlamini.

His family also testified that he also had the gift of healing. However, he often shelved this gift under the table. He told us that, he was concerned that people were going to come to church for the wrong reasons; for physical healing (which is temporary) not for spiritual nourishment (which is eternal).

Late in the years when his physical strength began to fail, Rev. Mnisi remained dedicated to his call. His daughter, Maggie, once took him to a medical check-up with their family doctor in Manzini. After the medical examination the doctor advised him to slow down. The doctor said "Mkhulu your results suggest that you need to cut-back on your pastoral activities." Maggie recalled that these words were followed by a long moment of silence in the consultation room. After a while, Mnisi said: "*Cha ngiyakuva mntfwanami, kepha mine ngibitelwe kushumayela. Ngitawumiswa nguNkulunkulu.*" He understood the doctor's concern, but he had resolved to work up to the last moment when God calls him home.

He loved the Lord and working for Him. Indeed, God was faithful to his servant, He called him to come back home directly from the pulpit.

.

Chapter 9

A perspective on tithes and offerings

> *"Let him who is taught the word share in all good things with him who teaches. Do not be deceived, God is not mocked; for whatever a man sows, that he will reap (Galatians 6: 6-7).*

The church of the Nazarene in Africa was launched by Rev. Harmon Schmelzenbach, commonly known as *Sibhaha* (bitter herb). He was supported financially by the Foreign Mission Board and the Women's Foreign Missionary Society (now Nazarene Missions International or NMI). However, this support dwindled during the period of the First World War from 1914 to 1919. Things got even worse during the period of the Second World War from 1939 to 1945, when a large number of missionaries were recalled to their homelands.

During these times, the Church of the Nazarene in Swaziland had to look for local support. Tithing (the giving of one-tenth of one's personal income) became a life-line. Pastor Elijah Dlamini is reported to be the first person in the church to offer his tithes after he felt convicted about his lack of tithing in 1925. There after several young native pastors responded to his testimony and a revival caught on. In the 1950s, the tithing revival had spread nationally. The late Rev. Thomas Zameya Ndlovu was known to be a specialist on this subject [Dayhoff, "Ndlovu"]. He spread the tithing movement at Ensingweni, Endzingeni, and in Manzini. He was sought nationally to preach about it such that in 1964, he became the first full-time Nazarene evangelist in Swaziland. He preached on giving with humor. He is widely remembered for giving people names such as *"Khebeshe"* (One who cheats God on tithes) and *"Gubhela kwesakhe"* (One who is self-indulgent or greedy).

Rev. Mnisi also supported this movement. He recalled that in 1963, he once hosted a week long revival on the theme of "Tithes and Offering". That revival led to the birth of the pastor's box ministry *(inkonzo yelikhathoni)* that is today practiced in a number of churches. His favorite hymn for collecting tithes and offering was *"Ngenisani okweshumi kwaJehova* (Bring in the Sheaves)".

He believed that tithes and offerings were commanded by God to the Israelites and to the evangelical church. His perspective was that obedience leads to blessings. He therefore challenged both believers and non-believers to bring in the tithes so that their labor can flourish. He gave an example that a professing Christian who commits adultery automatically cuts himself off from the blessings of a happy marriage. A non-believer who obeys this commandment "**Thou shalt not commit adultery**" also receives the blessings of a happier home. Everyone gets rewarded for obeying the Lord's commandment.

He said that tithing is an act of acknowledging God's providence. It is also a way to check our greed and a good spiritual exercise. However, he was careful to separate tithing from the conditions for salvation. As Jesus also taught that the good act of tithing does not justify us before God (Matthew 23:23, NIV): "**Woe unto you, teachers of the law and Pharisees, you hypocrites! You give a tenth of your spices—mint, dill and cumin. But you have neglected the more important matters of the law—**

justice, mercy and faithfulness. You should have practiced the latter, without neglecting the former."

Rev. Mnisi not only preached about tithe but practiced it, even during his retirement. His daughter Jean reported that each time they gave him an allowance, he would say *"Awu nami sengitawutibekela [kweshumi kwaJehova]"*. Tithing was the first item in his budget list.

Chapter 10

Tribute from his Children

"You are our letter, written in our hearts and known and read by everyone" (2 Corinthians 3:2, ISV)

Maggie Mnisi: The one thing that stood-out from my father was love. He loved people. He loved his family. He used to say that we should love everyone because they were God's creation. My father used to carry two handkerchiefs in his pocket. One for his use and the other to clean children's faces. He enjoyed playing with children in the church. This was his way of humbling himself. We loved him so much. When we were young, he always kept his promise to discipline us when we had gone astray. My father also loved my mother so much. We saw him pampering my mother every day. Some of us rushed into relationships just to taste the love my mother received from him.

My father also had a gift to see things before they happen. In his last days, he told me what was going to happen in my family. He said I should not be surprised but I should rely on God for support. Indeed these things came to pass and I am not moved, I have peace with God. My father is my true hero.

Jean Mnisi: I remember my father for his humility. He always began his day with a prayer at 5 AM. He prayed inside his bedroom, his prayers were refreshing. He opened our home to everyone: missionaries, pastors, and to people from all walks of life. We used to call his car the *imoto yemgcwabo* (hearse). He would volunteer with his car to carry coffins to the cemetery for poor families who cannot afford to rent a car. He led funeral services even for non-members of the church. He taught us to love people because they are an image of God. He also tried to balance family and his ministry.

In 1994, when I lost my husband, my father came to comfort me. He said I can remarry because I was young. But I can also concentrate on raising my children. He was open about my situation and promised to support me all the way. He loved my mother; they loved each other so much. They never argued in front of us. When we brought food home, he would bless it in front of us. I will always remember my father as a humble man. The last meeting I had with my father, he asked me read the scripture, 2 Timothy 4: 1-5, as his final message to his fellow pastors

Dumsile Magagula: It is really difficult to find suitable words to describe my grandfather because he was a perfectionist. He was all a child could ask for from a parent: a true father figure, a role model, a genuine man of God, and a devoted Christian

My grandfather was a true father figure to his own children, grand-children, great grand-children, relatives and to everyone. He taught us true Christian values because he lived by them. He lived as though he never sinned (I am not exaggerating). He stood firm in what he believed in. I remember when it was time for the reed dance (*umhlanga*), he would rather pay the required amount of money than for us to go there.

He loved and cherished our friends, my dearest friend Tricia Nothstine can attest to this. He taught her to eat Swazi food especially *ligusha*, and he loved her dearly. He gave each and every one of his grand-children names; we still use them even today. He was faithful in using those names when calling or addressing us. One other thing I will cherish for as long as I shall live is that he was faithful in praying for us. He would call us name by name and ask GOD to protect us physically, emotionally and spiritually. He did this faithfully until some of us got married. He would pray for our partners as well. He is greatly missed even today. Not a single day that passes without thinking about him. When we are gathered at home, we would say *"kube kuna Mkhulu nyalo ngabe sewutsi."* His legacy will forever live in my heart and mind.

Khetsiwe,Nomsa, Bongani, Thuli, Nicholus, Lindiwe, and Vusi: When we grew-up our younger father Caiphas would often come to our home to visit his brother. They loved each other and they were inseparable. They shared everything, even a plate of food. When our father passed away, our Rev. Mnisi became the only father we had. He was the stronghold of the family. He wanted all the children in the extended family

to be united.

Even though we go to different denominations, when our uncle was around he would teach us hymns from the Church of the Nazarene such as *"Kanye nawe Nkhosi yami."* We cherished every moment. He taught us to be respectful. He reminded us to honor our family name: *Mnisi, Mvulane--* the rain makers. He also taught us to dress with modesty. He said that girls should not wear trousers because when the angel of the Lord visits them, He would be confused if one is a boy or a girl. Thus girls who wore boy's clothes will miss out the blessings of a having children.

He warned us to avoid family disputes. He told use when we are at each other's throat a stranger would use that opportunity to rob us our father estate.

Chapter 11

Tribute from the Church

"Beloved, do not imitate what is evil, but what is good. The one who does well is of God; the one who does evil has not seen God"
(3 John 1:12)

(i) Mrs. Elsie Gamedze (Siteki Church of the Nazarene): Mkhulu Mnisi is a legend; he left a legacy of hope to most of us. He died pure, having fought a good fight. He unleashed his best work for Jesus Christ, our Lord. He was indeed a devoted man of God. He inspired everyone as a great example in the society. He taught us that the impossible is possible with God! He was a God fearing man, down to earth and never judgmental. He was a pastor, a father, a grandfather, and a friend to most of us. We will always remember his words: *"Sitawufika ekuseni eSangweni."*

(ii) Rev. T. Nothstine: We remember Rev. Mnisi as a dedicated servant of God. He was so much like the Lord. He preached like a prophet with fire in his bones. He planted

many churches, like the apostle Paul. He was a leader with words weighed carefully. His words carried a decision making persuasion. We learned so much from him as new missionaries. We appreciated him as a pastor, church planter, and evangelist. He was a pattern that we were fortunate to have at Siteki Bible College Church.

(iii) Mr. Bulunga: I first met Rev. C. Mnisi in 1979 at Mafutseni Nazarene Primary School, where I was teaching together with his daughter Jean. In 1981 when I came to teach at Siteki Nazarene, he became my pastor. Interestingly, he registered me as member of the church without waiting for my transfer letter from Sharpe Memorial Church of the Nazarene. From 1981 to 1989, I worked closely with him. I would go with him whenever he went for hospital visitations at Good shepherd. The Mnisi family has helped me in my Christian walk. Both *babe* and *make* Mnisi practically demonstrated holy living.

As a young man, he taught me to get the truth before doing something; that I should be quick to listen and slow to speak. Rev. Mnisi often said *"Manibusiswe nguJehova."* Lately, I have gained a clear understanding of the expression. I now often use it to bless other people.

(iv) Dr. Charles Gailey and Mrs.Gailey: We first met Rev. Mnisi when he came to Siteki to speak in revival services at Fitch Memorial Church in the early 1960s. The revival was wonderful and many people found help in their Christian walk. Later, after Pastor Leonard Sibandze was elected District Superintendent, the Church called Rev. Mnisi from Johannesburg to become Pastor. Rev. and Mrs. Mnisi quickly endeared themselves to all of us who lived at Siteki. He was a powerful preacher, but he was much more than that--he was

an upright, moral man who "walked the talk". He was a man of prayer. He was our friend. They were a powerful influence on our children--our son told Rev. Mnisi once that one reason that he was so blessed as a teenager is because, "I sat under your ministry!" And Make laMsibi was always by his side in the Lord's work. The Mnisi family has blessed our lives. We will always remember them!

(v) Rev. Ellen Gailey Decker: As a child growing up in Siteki, Swaziland, some of my earliest memories are of Umfundisi and Make Mnisi. I don't remember any individual sermon I heard from Umfundisi Mnisi, but I do remember the message they lived out with their lives: love God above all, love others above self. Alvinah Dlamini was a wonderful person who worked in our home, but she had a sister who was a drunkard. But when Reginah became saved, her life was totally transformed. Umfundisi Mnisi, as her pastor, mentored her and helped guide her in how to do visitation and personal evangelism. Reginah had a great ministry to many before she passed away. A missionary friend's kid, Dan Miller, was named Jabulani Mnisi after Umfundisi Mnisi. Dan was proud to be named after a man of

integrity and honor.

I was privileged to see the Mnisis on trips back "home" to Swaziland in 2000, 2003, 2008, and 2010. Every time, Umfundisi Mnisi was courteous and welcoming. Mrs. Mnisi always welcomed us with open arms, a warm smile, and a twinkle in her eye. Both of these saints of God enriched my life by modeling Christ-like living to me as a child, and by being excellent role models in my adult life.

(vi) Siphiwe Carol Gailey Holt: For most of the time that I lived in Siteki during Rev. Mnisi's tenure as pastor there, I was away at boarding school or college and only was able to attend church services when I was home on holidays. So, it was while I was on holiday one year that he preached a powerful sermon on sanctification and holiness, using Romans 12:1-2.

I went home and thought and prayed about those verses the rest of the day in my bedroom. It was that very evening that I prayed through, presenting my body and life as a living sacrifice, surrendering to God's will for me, accepting His supreme Lordship over my personal life and accepting the power of His Holy Spirit. What peace! My life has never been the same ever since and I owe a great debt to Mfundisi Mnisi and his obedience in preaching faithfully from God's Word.

I am looking forward to spending eternity with him and his sweet lovely wife.

(iv) Rev. Star Lukhele (Maternal nephew): I remember Rev. Mnisi as a loving pastor who accommodated all ages in his ministry. He had the habit of carrying two towels in his pocket, one for his use and the other one for children. He respected children. He was the pastor for everyone. He

strongly believed in the ministry of home and hospital visitations. He would attend funerals in the community for both members and non-members of the church. He attended community meetings at the Royal Kraal (*emphakatsi*).

Mnisi's sermons dwelt on the doctrine of Holiness. He lived what he preached. I cannot remember a single event where he compromised the message of God. He was sincere and lived by Faith until he passed-on. I am challenged by works he did for God. He touched the heart of God and led people back to Christ, built beautiful churches and left a legacy on the Gospel of Holiness. Even at his retirement he led the construction of one the most beautiful churches, the Mahenjane Church of the Nazarene.

Chapter 12

Tribute from the authors

> *"A good name is more desirable than great riches; to be esteemed is better than silver or gold"* (Proverbs 22:1)

Simiso and D.J. Shiba seated with Rev. Mnisi at his home. This happened to be last get-together meeting.	B. F. Dlamini seated with Rev. Mnisi and D. J. Shiba from left to right.

(1) B. F. Dlamini: I came to Siteki in 1998 to enroll as a student in the Diploma Program at the Bible College. I only

knew Rev. T. T. Dlamini who came from my local church and also happens to be part of my extended family. At first I was assigned to teach Sunday school among the children. I was shy and never liked to be noticed. We used to go to Fitch Memorial Church in the afternoon on Wednesdays and in evening service on Sundays. Most of the time we were there, *babe* and *make* Mnisi would be there too. I noticed quickly something about *Mfundisi* Mnisi who had retired by then:

a. Punctuality or time keeping. For some reasons it happened that they used to arrive earlier than most of us. Sometimes they would wait outside until the one with the key opened for them. They used to be reported in case they were not attending.

b. Respect and recognition. Mnisi was able to master our different surnames without confusing us. This set him out from the other elders in the church. For example, the then District Superintendent, Rev. John Malambe seemed to have a very poor memory on that aspect. Every time we greeted each other after church Mnisi would respond *"Yebo Nkhosi"* and to my surprise he also knew my grandmother and share brief stories about her. However, Rev. Malambe would greet and then ask, *"Kodwa uwakabani?"* until one day he was scolded by one pastor from the North District, *"Mfundisi, you mean awubati labantfu uhlala nabo laSiteki onkhe malanga."*

During those days I also realized two towards student-pastors:

(a) The keep a distance attitude-- Some accomplished pastors would look at you as a student from a distance. You earn their trust through good works. The moment you mess up they are fast to shut you up. This group once there is a

small mistake they sound the trumpet of disappointment and expulsion. Unfortunately, this attitude also dominates among pastors in the church even today.

(b) *We are all-together attitude--* Some accomplished pastors were more welcoming to the student pastors. This group had the attitude that since you say God called you, I will support you and trust you until you say otherwise. Mnisi had this attitude, he would never allow church members or even pastors to talk bad things about a fellow minister of the gospel. For those who made mistakes he used to say let us pray for them so that they realize their short comings.

I made a research on the module Pastoral Theology: whereby I had to interview Mnisi in his house as an experienced minister. I asked him the question what was your secret of success in ministry? He responded:

"I never and will never depended on others be it missionaries, fellow pastors, children, family or church leadership, but God alone. I allowed God to be the center of my life as a result when those who wanted to make me their part left, God raised or brought others to fix my problem. Most of those who failed in ministry were those who depended on others for their survival."

One day I was asked to lead the Wednesday prayer meeting. Mnisi noticed that I was shivering in front of the congregation. After the sermon, he came to me and said "I still shiver too every time I am asked to preach, you will get used to it." At my Graduation in 2003, Mnisi was asked to share words of wisdom. He encouraged us with the following words (2 Timothy 4: 2): **Preach the Word in season and out of season.** He emphasized to the graduates the value of preaching the word of God, not to focus on material gains or church politics.

I then left the East District and went to work fulltime in the North District. I was away from Siteki for two years 2004-2005. In 2006, I returned to Siteki mission to teach theology at the Nazarene College of Theology. We would sometimes meet the Mnisis especially *make* Mnisi since *mkhulu* was now attending Mahenjane Church of the Nazarene. In 2007 , I joined the East District to pastor Makhewu Church of the Nazarene. Now I had the opportunity to meet Mkhulu at pastor's meetings and district events. Now he was more of a colleague in ministry. Few things I learned as a leader:

(a). He was a straight-talker and persuasive in District meetings like conventions and district assemblies. At one point the District Sunday School president wanted to resign from serving in the position. Mnisi and others insisted that the officer return to the position. She finally did that.

(b). He openly raised his concern about the care of the ministers: he was worried about some pastors who did not have a shelter to hide their heads. At one gathering I recall him challenging the whole District to contribute towards the completion of Rev. P. P. Pato's house at Mzilikazi. Mnisi stated that God had asked him what he was doing about this issue. He then promised to contribute building material to roof at least one room of the uncompleted building. The event became emotional since Rev. Pato was present and cried as he received the donation of about E3000 as a special offering raised on that day. Mnisi pledged to give E500. My heart was moved by his generosity. Before Pato, died two rooms were roofed and plastered by Nicholus Dlamini and a group of youth from Simunye church of the Nazarene.

(c) Rev. Mnisi also did not shied away from any hot topic in church. He protested during the introduction of an additional 5.5 % collection from local churches to the District Budget. This meant the District collection from local churches had to rise from 30% to 35.5%. Mnisi said no to that and raised the fact that small churches with tiny budgets will fail to operate. He also suggested that he was going to take the issue to higher authorities if the District continued with the proposal. After a long discussion filled with emotions the District resolved to reduce the District budget by 4%. To this day, the East District Budget collects 31.5% from the tithes and offering in local churches, thanks to Mnisi's insistence that it be reviewed.

Personally, as a pastor I have learned a lot from his ministry and preaching style: his sermons were brief, encouraging, and straight to the point. He frowned at evil and loved everybody irrespective of statues.   He maintained a smile most of the time, even when he was reported ill. One day I greeted him and he responded, "I am fine, the clay is weak, but my soul is well." He envisioned heaven as a good place; he painted a good, vivid picture, about the Holy City. I will forever emulate that character.

On the last week before he passed on, I came across Mnisi along the eMasotjeni Road. It was a Thursday and we greeted as usual. He then asked how far we have gone with the data collection exercise for this project. I told him we were making some progress. He then asked about my colleague, Dr. S. K. Mkhonta, who was then in America. When I was about to leave him he insisted "Please make sure you finish the project even if I am no more because may be God loved that this book be published after I am gone." Tell your friend he might not find me, *setiyakhala tinkhukhu tasekhaya,* meaning that he was homeward bound. This was the last words I heard him say, and they were engraved in my mind as we were working on this project.

==================

(2) Simiso K. Mkhonta: I first met Rev. Mnisi in 1993 in a revival service at Makhewu church of the Nazerene. I was fourteen years old at that time. Our then local pastor Rev. D. Shiba (one of the author) had invited him as the speaker. He preached a sermon that transformed my life. It led me to develop a strong relationship with the Lord Jesus Christ from that young age up to this day.

I have to mention that I grew-up in a God-fearing family. For as much as I can remember, I knew that the fear of the Lord is the fountain of wisdom. I had felt though that there was a missing piece in my relationship with God. I was a camouflage Christian. My conduct and actions were to a large extent dictated by the environment, not by my faith. I carried the guilt for not being bold enough to stand-out from the crowd. I was following Jesus at a distance just like Peter at Jesus' crucifixion.

During the revivals Mnisi preached on sanctification. He said that Christ-likeness was the fruit of being filled with the Holy Spirit. It was not a human effort. He said we needed to bury our old nature. He told us the following story:

One day a farmer was growing cabbages. He noticed some piglets destroying his produce. He chased them away, only to see them returning after a short while. The second time, he was so furious that he literally threw each piglet over the fence in rage. His effort proved to be fruitless as they came back again after a short while. It was only after he had realized that their mother had all along remained inside the garden. His efforts were fruitless because he had missed the main problem, the old pig inside in the garden.

With this story Rev. Mnisi demonstrated that we needed to attend the root cause of our sinful nature. We need to crucify our old sinful nature and be filled with the Holy Spirit. After the brief message he invited us who wanted to be filled with the Holy Spirit to the altar with the song: *"Lophuzako kulawamanzi akomi cha, naphakadze cha!"* A vernacular song derived from John 4:14: **"Whoever drinks the water that I will give him will never be thirsty. The water that I will give him will become in him a well of life that lasts forever."**

I responded to the altar call and from that moment I had peace within me. I felt the assurance of being child of God.

Rev. Mnisi became my spiritual father. However, I did not have the opportunity to know him personally. I would see him during the annual District Camp meeting from a distance. In 2012 camp meeting, I remember seeing *mkhulu* and *gogo* Mnisi walking towards eNtamakuphila grocery. They looked frail but they were walking like young lovers. In my heart I had a longing that we needed to preserve the spirit these warriors! My first thought was that we needed to set-up a scholarship in honor of Rev. Mnisi to support student pastors at the Bible College. (I later found that God had planted the same idea with Rev. Harding and friends from her speech at

Mnisi's memorial service.)

In December 2012, I was at home from the USA where I was pursuing a research in computational physics. I was driving my local pastor Rev. B. F. Dlamini to his house. I cannot remember the subject of our conversation. I just remember suggesting that we write a book about the life of Rev. Mnisi. He embraced that idea since he also worried that the history of the church would be lost.

I then asked but how? He suggested that we talk to Rev. Shiba who is related with the Mnisis. Rev. Shiba was also for the idea and she said we can no longer let time slip away. She called Rev. Mnisi and arranged a meeting to see the following day. On the 22nd of December 2012, we met Rev Mnisi. He was also excited about the idea. He felt that his life story may bring others to the Lord. He began recounting his life experiences on that day.

After the interview he prayed with us. He asked God to bless this project so that lives can be encouraged and uplifted for the glory of God. I was so grateful to finally get the opportunity to meet the man of God who left a foot print in my life. At the same time I was fully aware about the huge task we had started. We also visited Rev. Mnisi on the 28th of December, 2012, for a second interview. This happened to be the last time I saw him. On these two occasions, I noticed that he was still the same person I had met about 19 years ago. He was still very persuasive in his speech, he often drag some words to capture your attention.

I believe that Rev. Caiphas Mnisi is one of the jewels that the bible refers to in Malachi 3: 17. I often wonder how Heaven would be. The thought has become much clear these days; Heaven is a fantastic place where we would meet our loved ones who have fought a good fight, including Rev. Mnisi. What a place it would be, *siyohlangana ekuseni eSangweni!*

================================

(3) Rev. Dumsile J. Shiba: I have known Rev. Mnisi from my early childhood as my maternal uncle. He was already a pastor when I was born. He used to visit my grandparents together with my aunt Mrs. J. Mnisi, every time they were in the country from Soweto. Since I was the only girl living with my grandparents, Mnisi allowed their daughter Jean to stay with me. Jean then went to school with me in Swaziland whilst her parents were in Soweto.

In 1969, the Mnisis returned to Swaziland to lead the Fitch Memorial Church in Siteki. Jean then moved to stay with her parents. I used to spend my school holidays in Siteki. After completing my high school education, I went to work in Siteki. I stayed at their home. In that midst I learnt that I was pregnant.

Rev. Dumsile J. Shiba preaching at Lubito Church of Nazarene.

I left the Mnisi family to live by myself in apartment as

a sign of respect to my uncle. He had warned us as children that he would not entertain us in the parsonage if ever we get pregnant before marriage. It was his way to discourage us from casual relationships. He was strict on this policy. Even his biological daughters had to leave the parsonage when they also got pregnant before marriage. My uncle did not compromise when dealing with matters of God. His character was a very important lesson later in my life. Even though he was strict on us, he loved his grand-children. He would say our children had not committed any sin. They were a precious gift from God. My uncle and aunt demonstrated their love when they adopted my one-month old daughter Lindumusa Linda Dlamini, who I had to leave behind when I went for my studies in Israel.

In 1985, God called me to ministry. But my employer, the Government of Swaziland, did not accept my resignation. I called my uncle to intervene. He travelled all the way from Siteki to my work place in the Hhohho region to pray with me. After a month, I was allowed to go to Siteki Bible College to pursue my training. Before I attended my first class, my uncle gave me this advice: Not to dishonor God and my parents in my ministry. He repeated the same advice after I had graduated. I was fortunate that I attended one of his classes at the Bible College. On Tuesday evenings, he used to lead a lecture on "Living a Holy life in your youth." On Saturdays at 8.30 AM, we used to gather for prayer with him. He then divided us into groups to visit homes around Siteki. He would also prepare a schedule for us to preach in the surrounding schools.

I would always remember my father as a person who stood for the truth. He taught us to be true in all things. He taught us as pastors to submit district budget as is. He also taught us to care for the other fellow ministers because we were called by the same God. I will never forget one incident when he shed tears in a pastors' conference. He told us that we had failed before God for not supporting a retired pastor who was struggling to complete his house.

This is the end!

To God be the glory.

============================

Bibliography

1. Dayhoff,"Vilakati." Dayhoff, Paul S. "Vilakati, Norman Magodzi" DACB. http://www.dacb.org/stories/swaziland/vilakati_norman.html

2. Dayhoff,"Mnisi." Dayhoff, Paul S. "Mnisi, Caiphas and Joan" DACB.http://www.dacb.org/stories/swaziland/mnisi-caiphas--joan.html

3. Gama, Loderick. "Notes." Siteki, 1992.

4. Dayhoff,"Ndlovu." Dayhoff, Paul S. "Ndlovu, Thomas Zameya, L."DACB.http://www.dacb.org/stories/swaziland/ndlovu_thomas.html

5. Dayhoff,"Ndlovu." Dayhoff, "Salome Khumalo."DACB.http://www.dacb.org/stories/swaziland/khumalo_salome.html

6. Enoch Litswele, *A memory of the Church of the Nazarene in Africa*, http://www.didache.nazarene.org/pdfs/AfrSpk-15_Litswele.pdf

7. Louise R. Chapman, *Footprints in Africa*, (Nazarene Pub. House, Kansa City, USA, 1959).

8. Gene Van Note, *The People Called Nazarenes: who we are and what we believe*, (Nazarene Publishing House, Kansas City, 1983)

Printed in Great Britain
by Amazon